A VISIT TO

Mexico

REVISED AND UPDATED

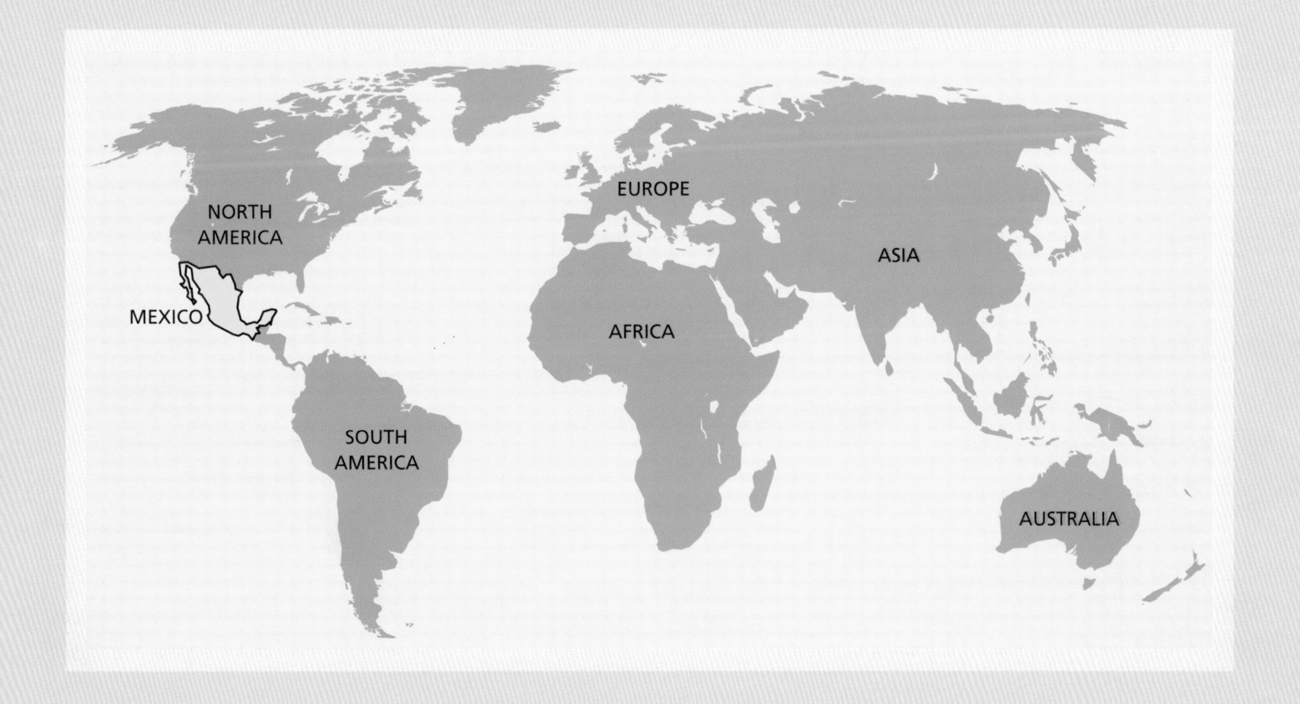

Rob Alcraft

www.heinemann.co.uk/library
Visit our website to find out more information about Heinemann Library books.

To order:
 Phone 44 (0) 1865 888066
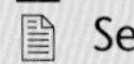 Send a fax to 44 (0) 1865 314091
 Visit the Heinemann Bookshop at www.heinemann.co.uk/library to browse our catalogue and order online.

First published in Great Britain by Heinemann Library, Halley Court, Jordan Hill, Oxford OX2 8EJ, part of Pearson Education. Heinemann is a registered trademark of Pearson Education Ltd.

Editorial: Diyan Leake
Design: Joanna Hinton-Malivoire and Philippa Jenkins
Picture research: Mica Brancic
Production: Duncan Gilbert

Originated by Chroma Graphics (Overseas) Pte Ltd
Printed and bound in China by South China Printing Co. Ltd

ISBN 978 0 431 087351 (hardback)
12 11 10 09 08
10 9 8 7 6 5 4 3 2 1

ISBN 978 0 431 087498 (paperback)
12 11 10 09 08
10 9 8 7 6 5 4 3 2 1

British Library Cataloguing in Publication Data
Alcraft, Rob, 1966 –
A visit to Mexico. – New ed.
1. Mexico – Social conditions – 21st century – Juvenile literature 2. Mexico – Geography – Juvenile literature 3. Mexico – Social life and customs – 21st century – Juvenile literare
I. Title II. Mexico
972'.0842

Acknowledgements
The publishers would like to thank the following for permission to reproduce photographs: © Alamy p. **24** (Marcin Mikolajczuk); © Getty Images p. **17** (Dorling Kindersley/Demetrio Carrasco); © Getty Images p. **5** (De Agostini Picture Library/DEA/S. Gutierrez); © Hutchinson Library pp. **7** (Edward Parker), **16** (Liba Taylor), **18**; © Link pp. **15** (Lourdes Grobet), **27** (Lourdes Grobet), **28** (Philip Schedler); © Panos Pictures pp. **12** (Liba Taylor), **22** (Sean Sprague), **23** (Liba Taylor), **25** (Sean Sprague), **26** (Sean Sprague); © Photolibrary pp. **8** (Jon Arnold Travel/Demetrio Carrasco), **10** (Robert Harding Travel/RH Productions), **13** (PhotoDisc/Keith Ovregaard/Cole Group); © Reportage pp. **19** (Julio Etchart), **29** (Julio Etchart); © Robert Harding Picture Library pp. **14** (Robert Francis), 20 (Robert Frerck); © Still Pictures p. **11**; © Telegraph Colour Library p. **6**; © Tony Stone Images p. **21** (Demetrio Carrasco); © Trip p. **9** (Ask Images).

Cover photograph reproduced with permission of © Lonely Planet Images (Brent Winebrenner).

Our thanks to Nick Lapthorn for his comments in the preparation of this book.

Contents

Mexico 4
Land 6
Landmarks 8
Homes 10
Food 12
Clothes 14
Work 16
Transport 18
Languages 20
School 22
Free time 24
Celebrations 26
The Arts 28
Factfile 30
Glossary 31
Index 32

Any words appearing in bold, **like this**, are explained in the Glossary.

Mexico

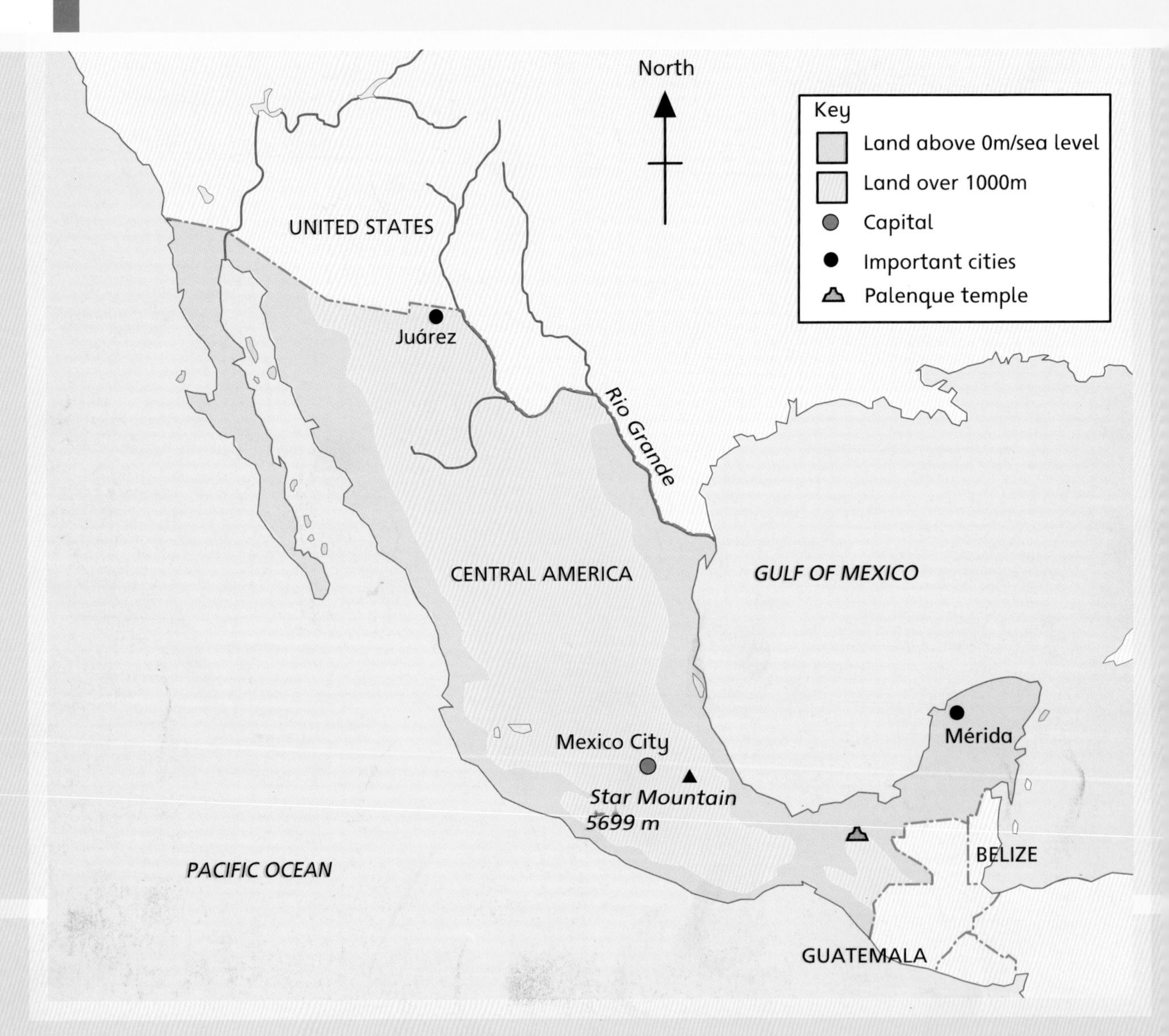

Mexico is a large country. It is in between the United States and the countries of Central America.

Mexico has many mountains. There are grassy **plains**, forests, and long beaches. Most Mexicans live in the warm, green **highlands**.

This town is in the Mexican state of Puebla.

Land

Mexico has hot deserts, where it is rocky and dry. Almost half of Mexico is desert. In some places it hardly rains at all.

High up in Mexico's mountains it can be cold. Star Mountain is Mexico's highest mountain. It is a **volcano**.

There is always snow on top of Star Mountain.

Landmarks

The **capital** of Mexico is called Mexico City. It is twice as big as London. There are 19 million people living in this big, busy city.

The temple at Palenque was built by people called the **Mayans**.

There have been cities in Mexico for thousands of years. At Palenque you can see a very old **temple**. It was once part of a great city.

Homes

Most Mexican homes are small. They might have two or three rooms for a large family. Grandparents, uncles, and aunts often live close by.

The whole family joins in the work in the countryside. They grow **maize** and beans to eat.

Homes in the countryside are like small farms.

Food

Mealtime is a time for the family to get together. People usually eat pancakes called tortillas with their meal.

Mexican food is often hot and spicy. The dishes may include chilli peppers and green peppers as well as avocados, beans, tomatoes, and herbs.

Clothes

Mexican children wear uniforms to school. In cities, Mexicans wear clothes such as jeans and baseball caps. Cowboy hats are popular.

Traditional clothes are hand-made and very colourful.

In the countryside, many Mexicans wear **traditional** clothes. Every part of Mexico has its own kind of clothes.

Work

Mexican workers make cars, machinery, and clothes. Other workers have jobs looking after **tourists**. They work in hotels and restaurants.

This farmer is working in a field of sugar cane.

Farming is hard work. Tractors are expensive so many farmers do a lot of the work by hand or they use horses.

Transport

Most people travel around Mexico by bus. The buses can get quite full as everyone piles their luggage on the roof and between the seats.

There can be a lot of traffic in the cities.

People often use horses and donkeys to carry things along small roads. Lorries and cars carry people and loads on big roads.

Languages

Mexico was once ruled by Spain, so most Mexican people speak Spanish.

People in the markets speak the language of the region they are in.

Many Mexicans can speak **native languages**, as well as Spanish. There are many different native languages spoken in Mexico.

School

All young people in Mexico go to primary school from age 6 to12. Not all children go to secondary school. Sometimes they leave to help their parents on the farm.

Mexican school children learn to read Spanish.

Mexican children study many subjects at school. Schools in the country have vegetable gardens where children also learn about farming.

Free time

Most Mexicans love football and basketball. They are played everywhere. There are **bullfights** too, which big crowds come to watch.

Lots of Mexican children help out at home when they are not in school. They might have animals to look after. It is work, but it can also be fun.

This boy is helping to milk a cow.

Celebrations

Every town and village in Mexico has its own **festival**. A band leads a parade around the street. Everyone dresses up, and there is a party and dancing.

The Day of the Dead is the time when Mexicans remember people who are dead. Families take presents to their **relatives'** graves.

The Arts

A lot of art in Mexico is made to be used, as well as looked at. People make pots and weave cloth. They use patterns that are very, very old.

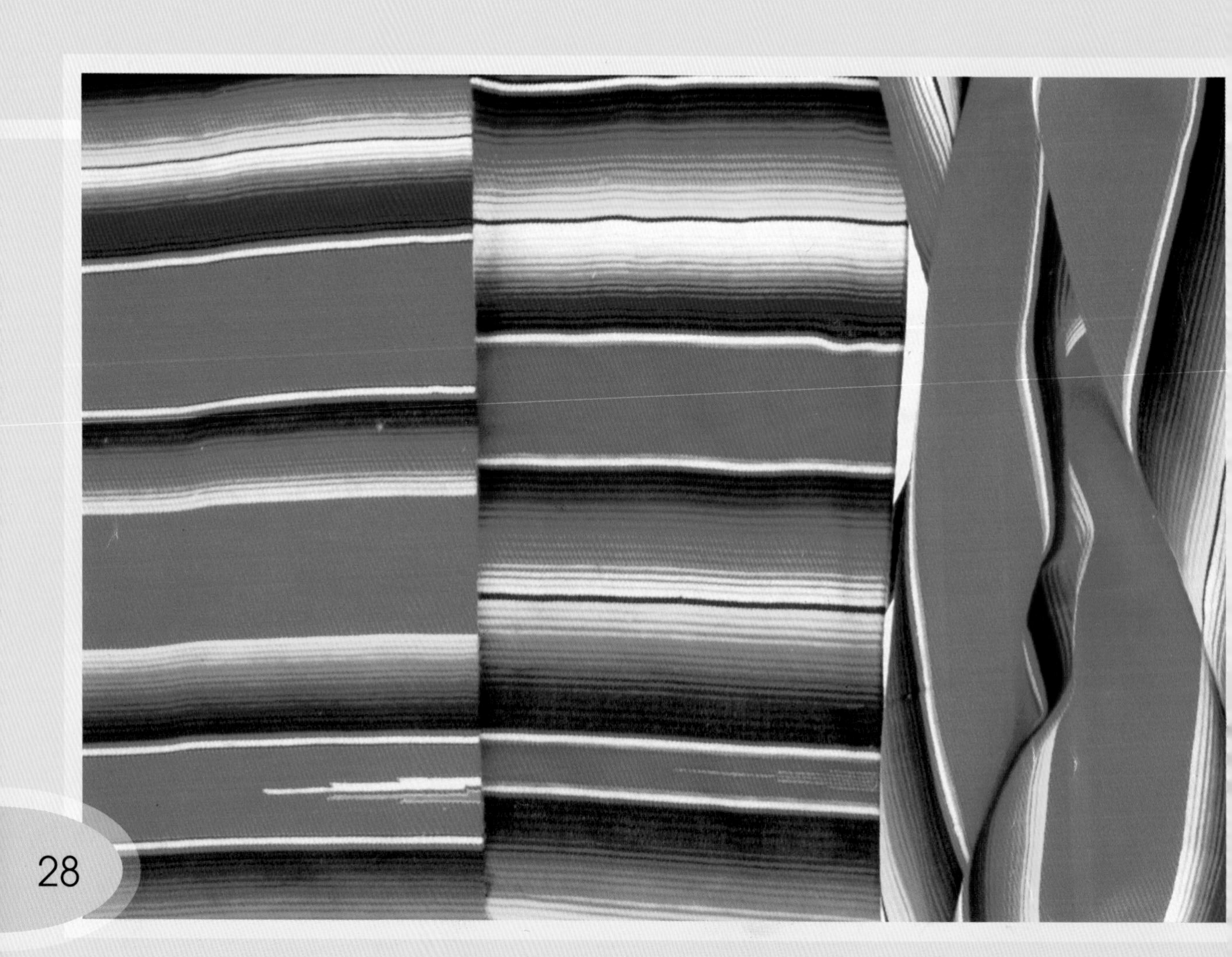

This massive mural is on a street in northern Mexico.

Mexican painters are famous for wall paintings. These paintings are called murals.

Factfile

Name	The full name of Mexico is the United Mexican States.
Capital	The **capital** city is Mexico City.
Language	Most Mexicans speak Spanish.
Population	106 million people live in Mexico.
Money	Mexican money is called the peso.
Religions	Most Mexicans are Catholics.
Products	Mexico produces lots of coffee, cotton, silver, oil and gas, cars, tinned food, and cloth.

Words you can learn

hola (o-la)	hello
adios (ad-ee-os)	goodbye
gracias (gras-ee-as)	thank you
si (see)	yes
no	no
uno (oo-no)	one
dos (doss)	two
tres	three

Glossary

bullfight a popular sport in Mexico and Spain. A bull is put in a ring and is made angry by people with swords on horseback. A person (usually a man) allows the bull to attack him and then he moves out of the bull's way

capital city where the government is based

festival party that a whole town or country joins in

highlands places where there are mountains

maize corn. In Mexico it is made into flour and used for breads and drinks.

Mayans a people who have lived in Central America and southern Mexico for over 1000 years

native language language that was spoken before people came from elsewhere and brought their own language

plains flat place, often covered in grass and shrubs

relative member of the family, such as a grandparent

temple special building used for worship, such as a church or mosque

tourist person on holiday in a foreign country

traditional the way things have been done or made for a long time

volcano a mountain or hole in the ground that sometimes throws out ash or melted rock from beneath the Earth's surface

Index

beaches 5

bullfights 24

Central America 4

Day of the Dead 27

deserts 6

farming 17

forests 5

highlands 5

Mayans 9

Mexico City 8

mountains 5, 7

murals 29

Palenque 9

peppers 13

plains 5

Spanish 20, 21, 23, 30

Star Mountain 7

tortillas 12

volcanoes 7